For Rosie
MJ

For Pippa—never stop exploring
VW

The author, illustrator, and publisher would like to thank Dr. Rosie Trevelyan of the Tropical Biology Association for her invaluable advice.

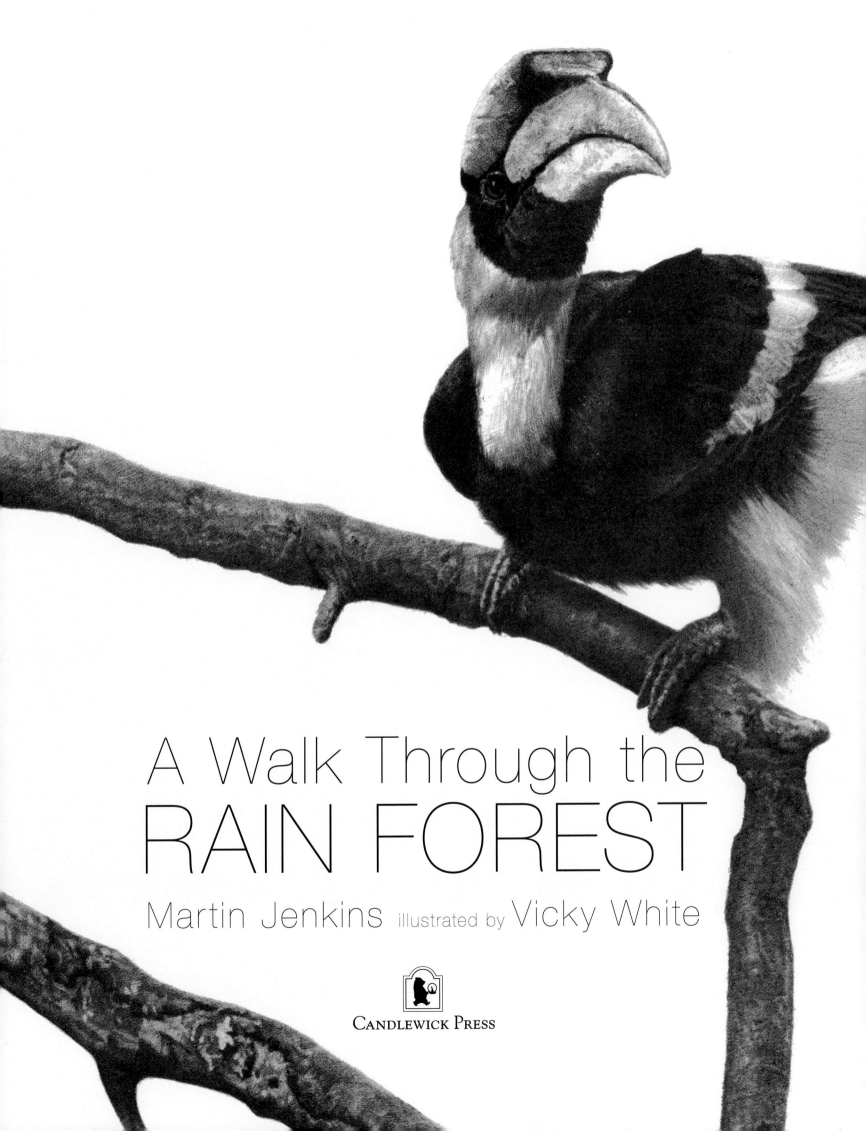

A Walk Through the
RAIN FOREST

Martin Jenkins illustrated by Vicky White

CANDLEWICK PRESS

Tropical rain forests are amazing places. More kinds of animals and plants live in them than anywhere else. This one is in Malaysia in Southeast Asia, in a place called Taman Negara.

Let's go and explore . . .

What's it like in here? Hot and sticky and pretty dark.

Where are all the animals?

There don't seem to be many, apart from a lot of ants and termites scurrying around.

This is a bit strange when you think that in this forest there are seven kinds of wild cats, six kinds of pheasants, twelve kinds of pigeons, at least fourteen kinds of squirrels, sixty-six kinds of frogs (more or less), eleven kinds of cuckoos, eighty kinds of bats (roughly), ten kinds of owls, nine kinds of hornbills, eighteen kinds of woodpeckers, hundreds of kinds of butterflies, goodness knows how many kinds of beetles (I certainly don't), and a whole lot more . . .

You may not be able to *see* many kinds of animals, but if you listen for a minute, you can *hear* plenty. That whirring is made by cicadas. The loud whistle is made by a well-hidden pitta. The chattering is a squirrel, though I don't know which kind. And that *woo-woo* is a great argus pheasant, a long way off.

I wonder if it's displaying to a possible mate . . .

So many animals, all
out of sight. But there
are some wonderful
things right in front of
us. Can you guess?

I'm talking about
the trees! They're
the biggest and the
oldest things here.
There are tons
of different kinds.
This one is called a
tualang. It must be
two hundred feet
(sixty meters) tall and
hundreds of years old.

But if you look around carefully, you might notice something a bit strange. All the trees here are big and old. There are no small, young ones. There are, however, small plants growing: mosses and ferns, sprawling palms called rattans, wild gingers, and arum lilies with dark, shiny leaves and weird flowers, but these won't grow into rain forest trees.

Eventually the big trees will die—they could be struck by lightning or be blown down in a storm or get a disease. But if there aren't any young trees growing around here to take their place, how will the forest continue to live?

Let's walk on to see if we can find some clues . . . .

Here's a giant fig tree with lots of fruit on it.

Now we can see some animals! They've come to feed on the fruit. Those large birds are great hornbills. And there's a family of gibbons and some fruit doves, too. That little bird with a big bill—I think that's a red-crowned barbet. All of them here to feast.

And there'll be others coming at night . . .

Here under the tree are lots of fallen figs. There are hoofprints, too, made by wild pigs. They love fruit but have to wait for it to fall to the ground before they can get to it.

Some of the figs have burst open. Butterflies are feeding on the sugary juices. Inside the figs are hundreds of tiny seeds. Any one of those could grow into a giant fig tree if it sprouted. Not here though—it's too dark. Like most forest trees, fig tree seedlings need lots of light to grow well. That's why there aren't any small trees around.

So where *do* they grow? Let's walk on a little farther to see if we can find out.

What's this? Some enormous footprints and a big pile of dung. The poop's still warm, which means whatever animal made it was here only recently.

It might be just ahead of us . . .

We've reached a clearing where it's much lighter. A huge tree fell, perhaps in a storm, and pulled down some of the trees around it—their tops would have been all tangled together with vines.

And there are young trees everywhere. *This* is where they grow—in gaps in the forest where sunlight reaches all the way down to the ground.

Each tree grew from a seed. But there aren't any trees with fruit nearby, so how did the seeds get here in the first place?

Look over there—
hornbills. They might
be the same ones
we saw at the fig
tree.

Oh! I think one of
them just pooped.

And here's
another pile of
elephant dung.

And I think that
pile is from a wild pig.

There's quite a lot
of poop, isn't there?
Let's take a closer
look at some . . .

The elephant poop is mainly brown and stringy—the remains of the leaves and branches that the elephant has eaten. But there are also some hard round things in it. They're durian seeds. Elephants are fond of durian fruit. And if we look in the pig poop or the hornbill poop, we'll find lots of smaller seeds, like the ones we saw in the figs.

This is how it works: many trees, like figs and durians, make tasty, sugary fruit that attracts animals, which eat the fruit along with the seeds. When the animals poop, with luck they'll poop out some seeds somewhere good to grow.

The poop helps in another way, too. Tree seedlings don't just need light; they need chemicals called nutrients that they take in through their roots. Often there aren't many nutrients in rain forest soil, but there's plenty in poop. So when a seed sprouts where an animal has pooped, it should find itself with a healthy supply of nutrients to give it a good start in life.

Of course it doesn't always work that way. Some animals, like parrots and squirrels, often chew up and destroy seeds instead of pooping them out whole. Some trees make seeds that are blown around by the wind. They don't need animals to carry their seeds, so they don't make any tasty fruit. And some trees have seeds that sprout into seedlings that can survive in dark places for years, until the trees above them fall down and make a clearing.

Whatever kind of seeds a tree makes, hardly any will grow into big trees; they'll rot or get chewed or end up in difficult places to grow. To make up for this, each tree produces huge numbers of seeds. With luck, some seeds will find themselves in a clearing like this, and a few of those will grow into saplings and then into full-grown trees. Eventually, in thirty or forty years, this won't be a clearing anymore . . .

This goes on all the time in the forest. Each of those big trees we saw will eventually die, and a new clearing will open up where it used to stand, ready for animals that have been feeding on fruit—perhaps from one of the trees that has grown up in this clearing.

And so the forest lives on. And that must be a good thing. Because without the forest, there would be nowhere for the seven kinds of wild cats, six kinds of pheasants, twelve kinds of pigeons, at least fourteen kinds of squirrels, sixty-six kinds of frogs (more or less), eleven kinds of cuckoos, eighty kinds of bats (roughly), ten kinds of owls, nine kinds of hornbills, eighteen kinds of woodpeckers, hundreds of kinds of butterflies, who knows how many kinds of beetles (I certainly don't), and countless other animals and plants to live.

And that wouldn't be a good thing at all, would it?

THE WORLD'S RAIN FORESTS

Equator

Taman Negara

This map shows the main areas where rain forests grow.

*T*ropical rain forests are found in parts of the world near the equator where it stays warm year-round and where there is a lot of rain. There are tropical rain forests in Africa, South and Southeast Asia (like Taman Negara), Central and South America, northern Australia, New Guinea, and Madagascar and on islands in the South Pacific and the Caribbean.

Tropical rain forests in different parts of the world

look very similar, but they have different kinds of animals and plants living in them. Nobody knows exactly how many kinds of animals and plants live in tropical rain forests altogether, but scientists do know it's a huge number. They think that between half and two-thirds of all the different kinds of plants and animals that are alive at the moment live in these forests.

People have cut down huge areas of tropical rain forest, mostly to grow crops and keep cattle. This has left all the living things in rain forests with less and less space. Many of them will go extinct if we keep cutting down the forests as fast as we currently are.

Some rain forests, like the one in this book, are protected in national parks (Taman Negara means "national park" in Malay), but not enough of them to make sure that all living things found in rain forests will be safe.

So many different kinds of animals live in
Taman Negara that we couldn't possibly
fit them all into this book. But we did
include a lot. Did you spot them?

**BLUE-CROWNED
HANGING PARROT**
Loriculus galgulus

BIRDS

GREAT HORNBILL
Buceros bicornis

HOODED PITTA
Pitta sordida

GREAT ARGUS PHEASANT
Argusianus argus

GREAT SLATY WOODPECKER
Mulleripicus pulverulentus

EMERALD DOVE
Chalcophaps indica

BROWN WOOD OWL
Strix leptogrammica

MALAYAN PEACOCK-PHEASANT
Polyplectron malacense

RED-CROWNED BARBET
Psilopogon rafflesii

WHITE-RUMPED SHAMA
Copsychus malabaricus

INSECTS and other INVERTEBRATES

A MILLIPEDE
Class Diplopoda

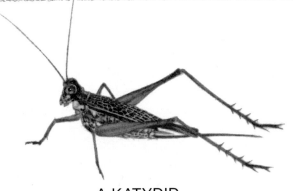

A KATYDID
Family Tettigoniidae

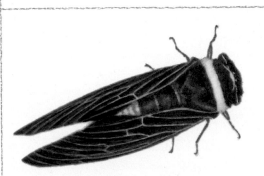

EMPEROR CICADA
Tacua speciosa

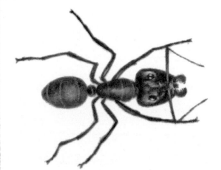

GIANT FOREST ANT
Dinomyrmex gigas

TERMITE
Macrotermes carbonarius

ATLAS MOTH
Attacus atlas

EMERALD SWALLOWTAIL
Papilio palinurus

LARGE TREE NYMPH
Idea leuconoe

GREAT MORMON
Papilio memnon

A DUNG BEETLE
Genus Onthophagus

ATLAS BEETLE
Chalcosoma atlas

MAMMALS

MALAYAN TAPIR
Acrocodia indica

BINTURONG
Arctictis binturong

CLOUDED LEOPARD
Neofelis nebulosa

ASIAN ELEPHANT
Elephas maximus

ASIAN TRI-COLORED SQUIRREL
Callosciurus prevostii

SUN BEAR
Helarctos malayanus

LAR GIBBON
Hylobates lar

LARGE FLYING FOX
Pteropus vampyrus

SUNDA COLUGO
Galeopterus variegatus

FROGS and REPTILES

DARK-EARED TREE FROG
Polypedates macrotis

TEMPLE VIPER
Tropidolaemus wagleri

BENGAL MONITOR
Varanus bengalensis

MORE INFORMATION

If you'd like to find out more about tropical rain forests online, the following organizations have good websites:

National Geographic Kids

Rainforest Foundation

World Wildlife Fund

World Land Trust

ABOUT THE CREATORS OF THIS BOOK

Both Martin Jenkins and Vicky White have a passion for animals that has taken them all over the world—Martin Jenkins in his work as a conservation biologist, and Vicky White in hers as a natural history artist.

Their first children's book, *Ape*, won the ASPCA Henry Bergh Children's Book Award, and their second, *Can We Save the Tiger?*, was a *Boston Globe–Horn Book* Honor winner. This is their third book.